TIME TO LEARN ABOUT
DAY & NIGHT

Pam Scheunemann

Consulting Editor, Diane Craig, M.A./Reading Specialist

Published by ABDO Publishing Company, 8000 West 78th Street, Edina, Minnesota 55439.

Copyright © 2008 by Abdo Consulting Group, Inc. International copyrights reserved in all countries.

Editor: Pam Price
Content Developer: Nancy Tuminelly
Cover and Interior Design and Production: Mighty Media
Photo Credits: Creatas, JupiterImages Corporation, ShutterStock

Library of Congress Cataloging-in-Publication Data

Scheunemann, Pam, 1955-
  Time to learn about day & night / Pam Scheunemann.
     p. cm.
  ISBN 978-1-60453-015-5
  1. Earth--Rotation--Juvenile literature. 2. Day--Juvenile literature. 3. Night--Juvenile literature.
  4. Time--Juvenile literature. I. Title. II. Title: Time to learn about day and night.
  QB633.S34 2008
  525'.35--dc22
                                2007030073

SandCastle™ Level: Transitional

SandCastle™ books are created by a team of professional educators, reading specialists, and content developers around five essential components—phonemic awareness, phonics, vocabulary, text comprehension, and fluency—to assist young readers as they develop reading skills and strategies and increase their general knowledge. All books are written, reviewed, and leveled for guided reading, early reading intervention, and Accelerated Reader® programs for use in shared, guided, and independent reading and writing activities to support a balanced approach to literacy instruction. The SandCastle™ series has four levels that correspond to early literacy development. The levels are provided to help teachers and parents select appropriate books for young readers.

Emerging Readers   **Beginning Readers**   **Transitional Readers**   **Fluent Readers**
(no flags)   (1 flag)   (2 flags)   (3 flags)

SandCastle™ would like to hear from you. Please send us your comments and suggestions.
sandcastle@abdopublishing.com

time

Time is an interesting thing.
You can't touch it. You can't
see it. You can't hold it.
But it is always passing by!

Time is measured in different
ways. Let's learn about day
and night.

time

The earth is always spinning. It takes 24 hours to complete one spin. It is daytime on the half of the earth that is facing toward the sun. It is nighttime on the half facing away from the sun.

New York and Hong Kong are on opposite sides of the earth. When it is 8:00 in the morning in New York, it is 8:00 at night in Hong Kong.

time fact

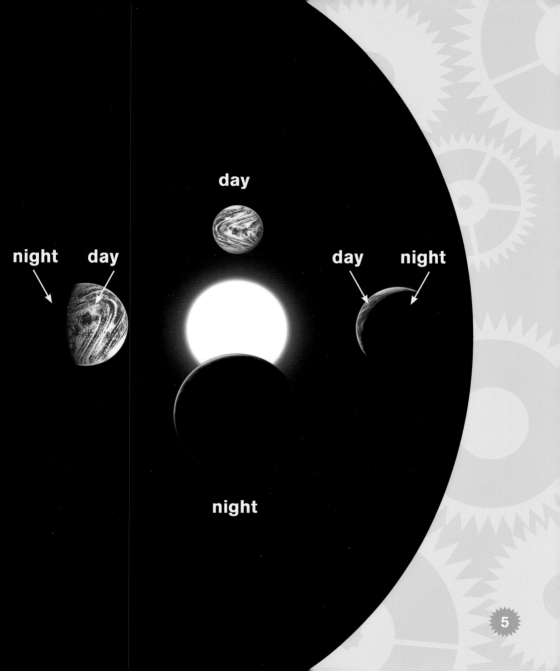

Each morning, David starts his day with breakfast. He likes cereal with milk.

The beginning part of each day is called morning.

day

People do things at certain times of the day. Tracy has computer lab at 11:00 a.m. each school day.

time fact

Times in the morning are called a.m. That stands for *ante meridiem,* which means "before noon."

Squirrels are very busy during the day. They play and search for food. Squirrels eat seeds, nuts, and fruit.

Animals that are more active in the day than in the night are diurnal.

time fact

midday

Noon is when the sun is at its highest point in the sky. Marshall eats lunch at noon. His favorite lunch is pizza.

Noon is also called midday or 12:00 p.m.

time fact

night

Julie does her homework in the evening before dinner. Her mom will help her if she doesn't understand something.

Evening is the end of the day and the early part of the night.

time fact

Jenna and her brother like to go to the beach at sunset. The sky becomes very colorful as the sun sets.

The sun sets in the p.m. That stands for *post meridiem*, which means "after noon."

Bats are busy hunting for food at night. During the day, they find quiet places where they can sleep. Bats hang by their feet and wrap their wings around themselves when they rest.

Animals that are more active at night than in the day are nocturnal.

Dee goes to bed at nine o'clock each night. She is asleep long before midnight. When she wakes up, it is a new day.

Midnight is 12:00 a.m. The date changes at midnight.

time fact

One way to think about time is in terms of day and night.

What things do you do every day or every night?

Before there were clocks, people used the position of the sun to tell time.

time fact